The official Baptism Book for Children

Yardenit - The Baptismal Site on the Jordan River

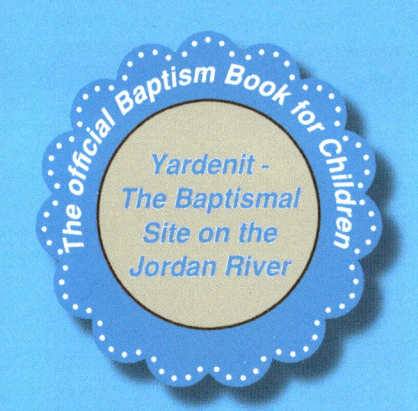

The Baptism of Jesus

A Story from the Jordan River

Jim Reimann

Illustrations by Najwan Zoubi

2

In the land of Israel, the holiest land of all,

There is a quiet, peaceful place, not too big or small.

"Yardenit" on the River Jordan is the place

Where over half a million come every year, by God's grace.

4

It is at Yardenit that people step into the river -
Hundreds of white-robed believers every single day.
Often the water is cool, so the people may shiver;
Still they come - to follow Christ in baptism and pray.

6

Pilgrim after pilgrim, from nation after nation,
Confessing and repenting of their sins and their wrongs,
Some in their ethnic garb travel to this location
To renew their faith, and sing sacred songs.

8

It was by this very Jordan - the River "Yarden",
With its holy water flowing so gently,
That John the Baptist had come to baptize - way back when,
For the river had much water - water aplenty.

10

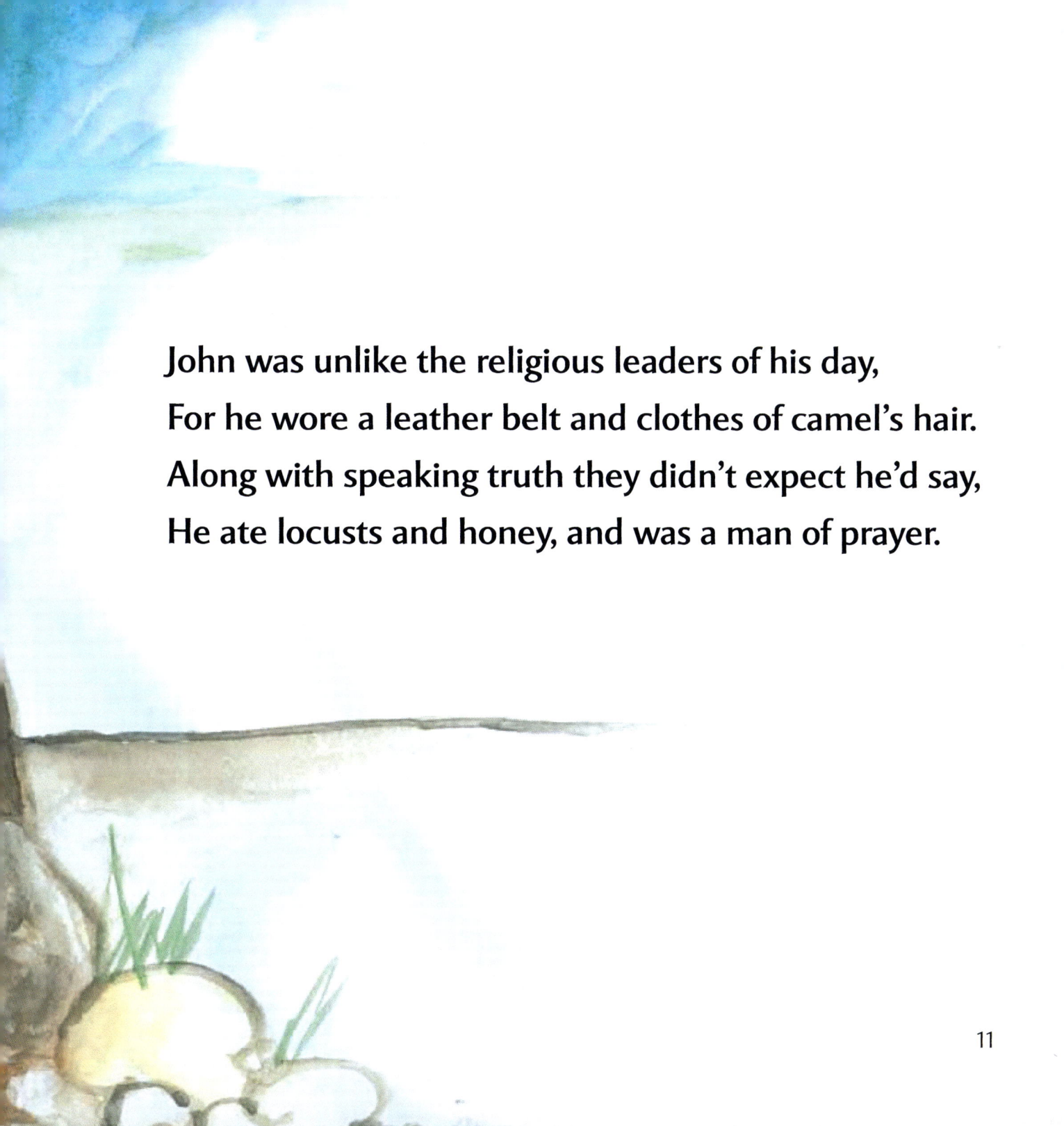

John was unlike the religious leaders of his day,
For he wore a leather belt and clothes of camel's hair.
Along with speaking truth they didn't expect he'd say,
He ate locusts and honey, and was a man of prayer.

12

There, close to the banks of the old Jordan River,
John preached, "Repent, for the kingdom of heaven is near."
He shared the words God had given him to deliver -
A desert voice calling out to those who would hear.

Many came, confessed their sins, and were baptized by John;
"I baptize with water for repentance," he told them all,
"But when the Messiah of God arrives," John went on,
"He will baptize with the Spirit, as you hear His call."

14

John was not the Messiah, as we know from God's Word,
For Isaiah foretold John would prepare Jesus' way.
And one day it happened by River Yarden - John saw the Lord.
Jesus the Christ walked straight toward him - this must be the day!

Yet John, a man whose heart was quite humble and contrite,
Felt unworthy to remove the sandals of the Lord.
But Jesus said, "Let it be so now, for this is right;
To fulfill what is said in My Father's Holy Word."

16

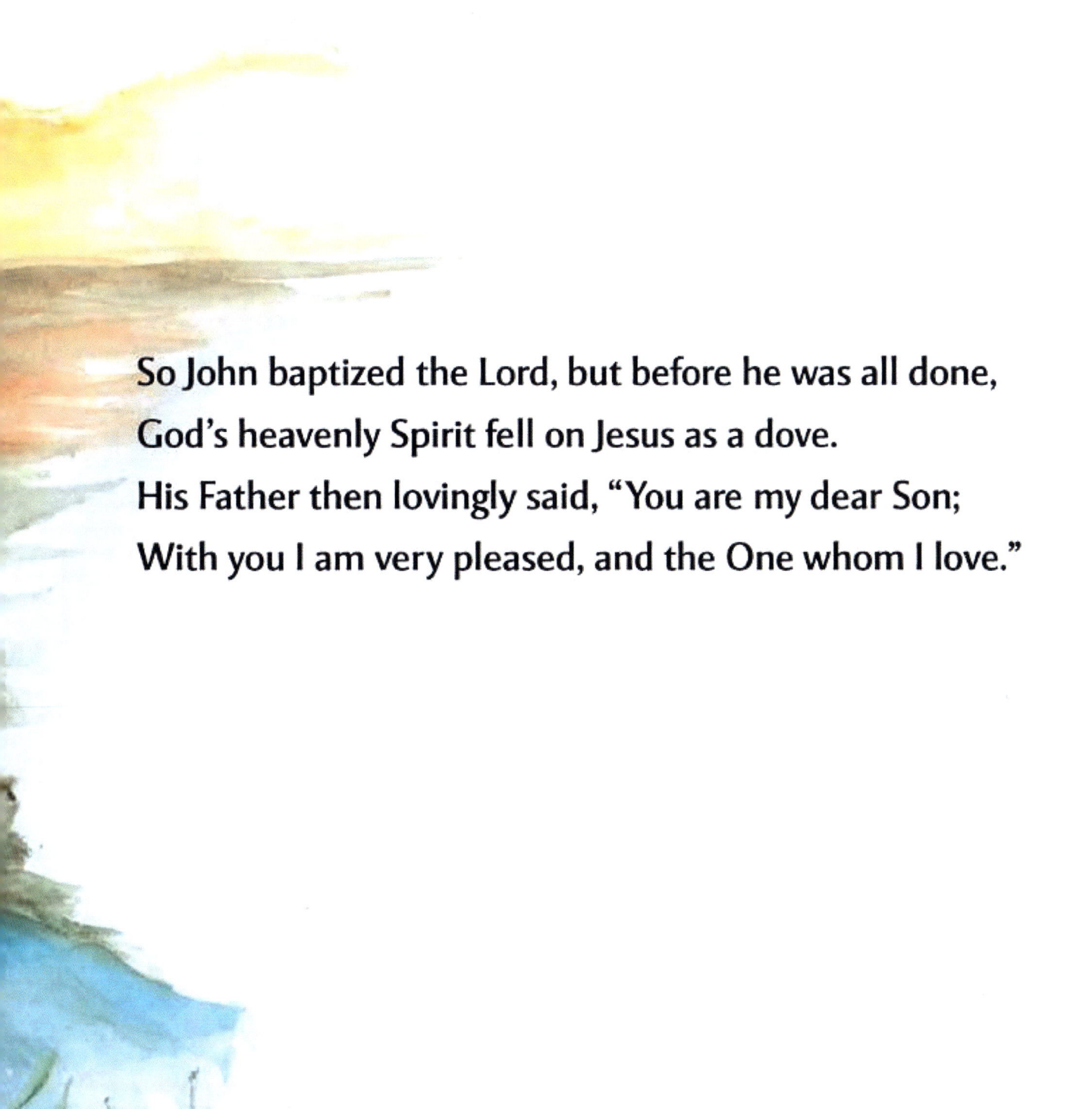

So John baptized the Lord, but before he was all done,
God's heavenly Spirit fell on Jesus as a dove.
His Father then lovingly said, "You are my dear Son;
With you I am very pleased, and the One whom I love."

18

It was then that Jesus began to preach the good news,
For the Lord's ministry began on that very day.
Speaking to all the boys and girls, Gentiles and Jews,
He said to be saved from sin, He alone was THE WAY.

20

Now there is a place on the River Jordan, "Yardenit" of today,
Where a great many come to baptize, sing and pray.
At "The Wall of New Life", surrounding the place so fair,
The ancient tale in more then 80 languages fills the air.

Yardenit -The Baptismal Site on the Jordan River

Over half a million Christians come each year from all over the world to visit Yardenit where they get baptized in the water of the Jordan River. Some are baptized for the very first time in their lives while others make a rededication of their life to the Lord.

The nature of the immersion in the living water at the Yardenit site is much like the Biblical immersion of the days of Jesus and his disciples. The waters of the Jordan River at Yardenit's area run clean and flowing, as it was in ancient times. The site was modified for the convenience of the visitors and their comfort, yet it retains its natural and primeval character.

After the immersion and ceremony, the pilgrims get a document called the "Certification of Baptism," a precious souvenir. Some pilgrims take home small bottles of water from the Jordan River as well.

The Yardenit baptismal site is rounded by a wall called "The Wall of New Life" which bears beautiful ceramic plates with the verses of Mark 1:9-11 in more than 80 languages and dialects. Also on site is a pastoral promenade which offers a tranquil intimate gathering place near the water.

What does the name "Yardenit" mean? The Hebrew name of the Jordan River is "Yarden" and the name "Yardenit" derives from it.

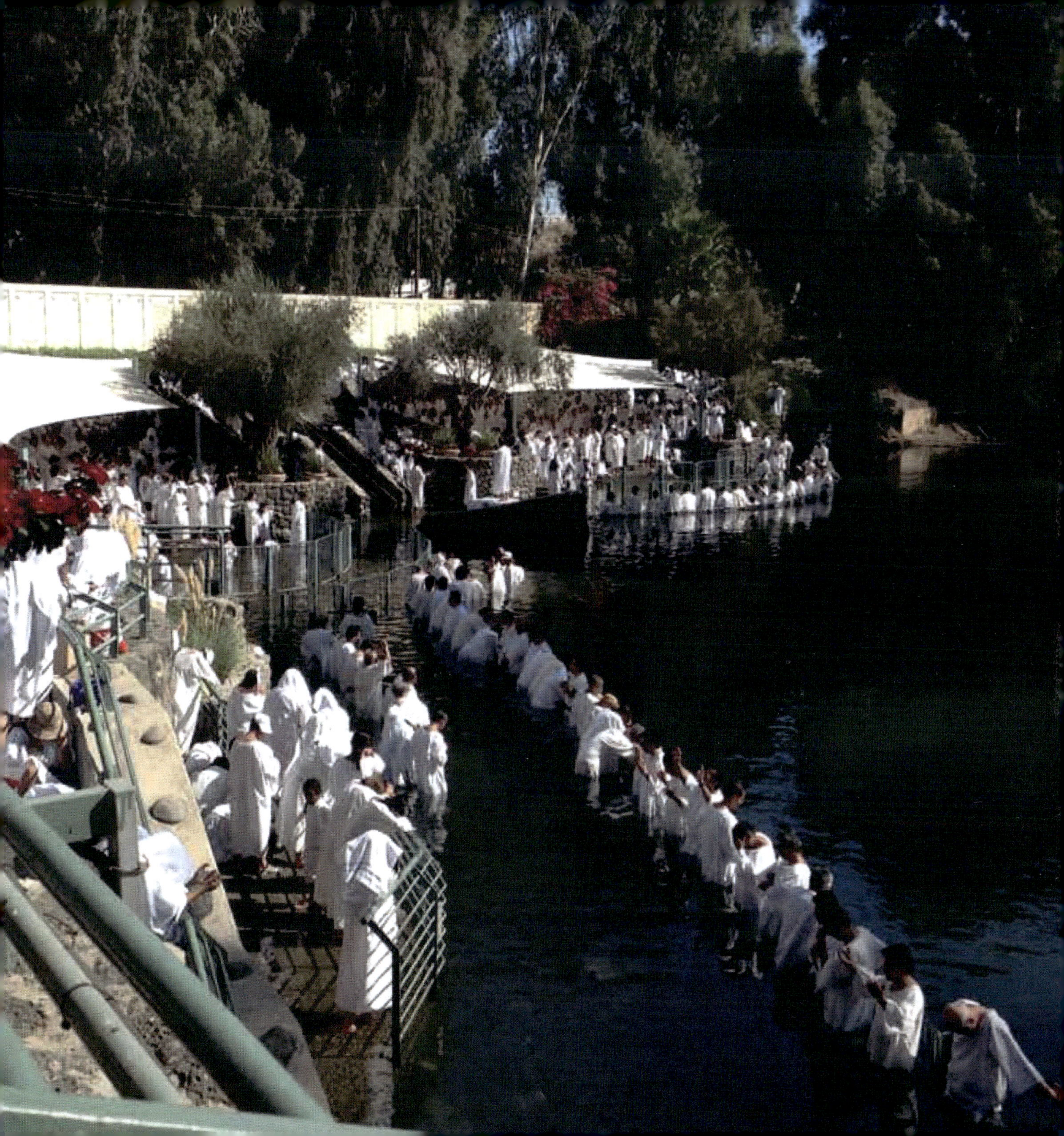

Intelecty L.t.d

Rev. Jim Reimann
Israel Tour Leader of 25+ Pilgrimages
Editor of the Updated Editions of:
My Utmost for His Highest (Oswald Chambers)
Streams in the Desert (Lettie Cowman)
Morning by Morning (Charles Spurgeon)
Evening by Evening (Charles Spurgeon)

All rights reserved. No part of the book may be used or reproduced by any means, graphic, electronic, or mechanical, including photocopying, recording, taping or by any information storage retrieval system without the written permission of the publisher, except in the case of brief quotations embodied in critical articles and reviews.

Printed by **GESTELIT**
info@gestelit.co.il
Printed in the Holy Land

Intelecty Ltd. Publishing House

Yardenit - The Baptismal Site on the Jordan River
- Free visit to the spiritual tranquil unique site
- Baptismal ceremonies
- Biblical Experience - film and lunch
- Souvenirs and Biblical gift shop

Open 7 days, 8:00 am to 17:00 pm
Tel. 972-4-6759111
E-mail: info@yardenit.com
Website and On-line Store : www.yardenit.com

The site of Yardenit was built by the Israeli Ministry of Tourism and functions as an official baptism site

Printed in Great Britain
by Amazon